BACKBONE

ESSENTIAL POETS SERIES 315

Canadä

Guernica Editions Inc. acknowledges the support of the Canada Council for the Arts and the Ontario Arts Council. The Ontario Arts Council is an agency of the Government of Ontario.

We acknowledge the financial support of the Government of Canada.

Praise for *Backbone*

"Now, the year opens like a sign, ready for iterations," writes Meryem Yildiz, her words a compass, language like symmetry that rolls off one's own feeling and emotion, profound and rightly clarifying. The book is layered, sultry and queerly erotic; it's tactile in its longing. She writes, "how it absorbed the tangy sweat of your arched, flushed forehead like a sea sponge." The words drip with ease, with potency, and we are brought into her Cancerian world of shelter and ballads about love. *Backbone* is now a favourite, I will return to this book again and again. I'm a Yildiz fan now.

—Fariha Róisín, author of *How to Cure a Ghost, Who Is Wellness For?* and *Survival Takes a Wild Imagination*

The poems in Meryem Yildiz's dazzling debut, *Backbone*, traverse the intersections of queer friendship, chronic pain, dreaming and waking life. They move between exterior and interior landscapes, from the "deep green veins" of the day as it "finds its way to midnight." There is a sense of telescoping backwards over a life in order to find meaning both in the paths taken and not taken. Pushing against the limits of this double life, Yildiz's speaker asks: "Who am I if I don't recognize myself?" This collection seeks to answer this question by recognizing the various forms of home and elsewhere that make up immigrant and female experience. "I left a world too," Yildiz's speaker addresses the reader: "we can learn together."

—Kasia Van Schaik, author of *We Have Never Lived on Earth*

I want to offer line after line out of *Backbone* to tell you how beautiful it is. Meryem Yildiz writes, "the paper bends, you lean out of / yourself," and we bend too, like grass, "in every blade / the ability to live." Her poetry is filled with lush rhythms, glistening with both pain and hope, "the white noise of your body crackling heedless." I am in awe of these poems, their wondrous language, and how they evoke all the complicated sensations of being alive, looking for kinship, brimming with possibility.

—T. Liem, author of *Obits.* and *Slows: Twice*

Richly interiorized, Meryem Yildiz's debut collection is a brave, intimate, absorbing meditation on human connection, chronic pain, and the complexities of identity. *Backbone* gifts us the full range – from narrative, breathy poems to shorter, more compact ones – in a language lush and fertile. Each poem is like another onion layer peeled back on vulnerability; taken together, they take us on an emotional journey toward a powerful message of healing and hope, of "elsewhere beckoning." My advice to you: read it slowly; savour these poems of the heart and mind—complex, sensual, and deftly executed.

—Carolyn Marie Souaid, author of *This Side of Light: Selected Poems (1995-2020)*

MERYEM YILDIZ

BACKBONE

GUERNICA
EDITIONS

TORONTO • CHICAGO
BUFFALO • LANCASTER (U.K.)
2025

Guernica Founder: Antonio D'Alfonso

Michael Mirolla, editor
Cover and interior design: Rafael Chimicatti
Cover image: *Study of Thistles*, Sophia L. Crownfield

Guernica Editions Inc.
1241 Marble Rock Rd., Gananoque, (ON), Canada K7G 2V4
2250 Military Road, Tonawanda, N.Y. 14150-6000 U.S.A.
www.guernicaeditions.com

Distributors:
University of Toronto Press Distribution (UTP)
5201 Dufferin Street, Toronto (ON), Canada M3H 5T8
Independent Publishers Group (IPG)
814 N Franklin Street, Chicago, IL 60610, U.S.A.

First edition.
Printed in Canada.

Legal Deposit – Third Quarter
Library of Congress Catalogue Card Number: 2024945644
Library and Archives Canada Cataloguing in Publication
Title: Backbone / Meryem Yildiz.
Names: Yildiz, Meryem, author.
Series: Essential poets ; 315.
Description: Series statement: Essential poets series ; 315
Identifiers: Canadiana 20240454898 | ISBN 9781771839532 (softcover)
Subjects: LCGFT: Poetry.
Classification: LCC PS8647.I43 B33 2025 | DDC C811/.6—dc23

For those who mend
and those who help mend

but when their rhythms
mesh
then though the pain of living
never lets up

the singing begins.
—Denise Levertov

Step into the Path, bring your branded heart,
for true lovers know each other by their scars.
—Attar

CONTENTS

I.

II.

III.

IV.

I.

Woman at a Window

after Caspar David Friedrich

in a way, we are all standing in, looking out.
we are all tilting to the left of the frame,
blood orange breath pasted on blue green
walls, fingers running to a tremble of oil
and vinegar. we are slanted for the long
golden aftermath of sunlit trees and
their tricky leaves, leaving. we cough
up the truth for a chance to vanish
in white skies, ivory hairpin flung
to the floor, collar cinched to mouth,
without so much as a sound goodbye.

Exit Strategy

when i peel off the door hinges and step outside,
my skirt lifts as an exit reminder: there is nothing
beautiful under the billowing wind. the air is filled
with pinpricks. i crawl on shorelines to see how
long it will take for fingers steeped in mud to stop
searching for a slant in the land. i clutch one half
of a heart that swells like a wave and release it,
watch it sink. i think, how easily barriers are crossed
through porous bones. but i do not seethe with blade
and blossoms between my teeth, i do not chastise
my own beating body divided into borrowed land.
have you looked at the life you made for yourself?
moments consumed at the small of my wrist, skin
silkened through countless years of rubbing.
i never know what it is i am polishing—blood
or rust, all this life beneath wings.

A Sheltering Place

i have a large kitchen island.

friends have commented on it behind my back.

“such a large kitchen island, gone to waste.”

i wouldn’t say i misuse it. there are salads, the occasional soup—meals of leafy greens and powerhouse vegetables to keep me safe or, at the very least, provide me with the illusion of protection from a sense of unease locked in disease.

i wash a kale leaf in the sink, press my thumb on the stem, release it of any dirt.

keep everything clean, i think, though i wish for soil underneath my nails, some kind of proof that this body ever touched the earth.

i watch as lumps crumble, fall and disappear into the water.

their path is one i cannot trace with a finger.

kale came to me by way of the mediterranean coast, thousands of years ago.

my father was of the same sea, but he left so i could grow up by a river whose current carried wide fragments of ice downstream. as a child, i watched them float by, dreaming of a life of carefree sailing on wandering islets made of snow.

now, the year opens like a sign, ready for iterations.

i remember this as i wrap myself in the kale's curling leaf, ground my fingers underwater in a stream of vanishing earth, and anchor in for months of stillness and waiting.

kale can withstand the cold.

we'll survive the journey.

The World Begins Here

saliva starts, dark sun arms

the warmth of her body

giver of care, mother divine

the taste of god in our mouths

the word begins, fulfills

fills up, gentle static incisors

mouth shut save for a slit

she said, drink slowly

mind open, tender baby belly

elixir of life inhaled

that first taste

of sweetness

a sip of blood-warm milk

In Other Words

at times i am the liver of my father's soul,
canımın ciğeri, or my mother's sweet heart,
cocotte, a woody cone plucked from a pine tree.
i learn to withstand contrasts early on from
one sentence to another. *yüzünü yıkadın mı*?
yes, i washed my face. *peux-tu mettre la table,*
la grande? of course, five forks in hand.
when i struggle to finish my *patlıcan*, the slime
of stuffed eggplants doused in garlic and oil coiling
on my plate, i eye the copper ayah hanging above
the kitchen table: *yiyin için israf etmeyin* çünkü
allah israf edenleri sevmez. that's a mouthful,
but who would condone the wasteful? certainly
not god. and as the words loom over me,
i cannot bear to disappoint him either.

Bois de Belle-Rivière Regional Park, c. 1987

for Osman

the three of us, a syzygy in a trail of muddy leaves.
we are our mother's earthly bodies, a concatenate
of red and blue raincoats. behind me, our brother,
all set, hands folded under his armpits, elbows
spread out like wings. i dance too, standing on one foot
in rubber boots, ready to go. you don't quiz any of this
with phosphenes and brushfield spots in your baby
brown eyes, fat tongue sticking out. you clasp
your small hands—the smallest of hands—
and hide your sweet flat face, because you do not
understand to look at the camera when maman asks
us to smile. instead you gaze into a grey stone well,
chirping in a language only squirrels would know.
maman brought us here to see the leaves change.
we smile for her with skinny trees and tight fists,
your unfathomable mind in kinship with groundwater,
the extra chromosome in your palm holding us all
together.

Pocket Knife

my father prays so much there are sunken
indents in his prayer mat. between salahs
he moves from left to right, to even it out.
he lives in those hollows, studies them with
his knees, his hands, his implacable forehead.
an expert in routine, stable footprints, in prostra-
tion to the most merciful, always seeking mercy.
i don't understand where he gets his faith, this man
with a pocket knife so sharp it could kill a man,
this man who never knew the meaning of comfort.
some foggy mornings, he pulls out the blade,
peels bright oranges in long broad strokes. how
can a blade that releases the sun also threaten
a rival in the boiler room of a norwegian ship?
the thought of it—the pocket knife in his pocket
or under the phone, next to the nail clipper in the
mahogany buffet drawer. a means to cut unruly
strands, some more rind, some more man,
to cut the dark out, to find the light.

Hawā

she is nameless, the mother of mankind. her gaze
sullen and fickle, distracted body covered with
a jagged green thing. she is trying to tame her toes,
avoid a flighty collision with flowers.
he's there too, of course. don't let anyone fool you:
he's the one holding temptation as the fountain rustles.
we all know his name, but why say it at all when
the nameless burns a hole in my pelvis, her voice
untold in the book i'm not allowed to touch so long
as my sullied body sheds non-creation.
mother of mankind, i am not told your story—
tall figures above me more concerned with what
i cannot eat, which foot to step with first (right),
what sacred phrase to utter at the kitchen table.
but here's the secret: snacks aren't meals, so when
i bite into an apple, body full of blood and abandon,
i forget the *bismillah*. the great forgiver might just
have better things to do than mind a child
poking holes in her own story.

Painting Jahannam

sometimes it's okay to let go of the reins
and trust in the skills of deft hands,
their leaden or feathered strokes.
i am an inanimate thing, first and foremost,
before i become pressed against the canvas,
turned into fire features, misplaced eyes.
these hands make a hell out of my pains and
aches, red mud deepening in the mangrove
trees, breaking the flood. despite so many
liquid vices tempting my good spirit body,
i do not drink from the murky river. i am oil
in gold-mines. i withstand the flames. i trim
these hands until they are fingerless palms,
emptied of me.

Immolation

hush, in immolation, a faithful flame makes
no sound. i don't consume myself so lightly.
i prefer a slow burn: steady as i go, winning
the race in stillness. in my bedroom, i strike
a match. what if i swallowed it? opened my
red mouth and let the fire coat me all the way
down. please, don't ruin it for the rest of me.
i paint myself charred, for the soot. i make
the sacrifice. i could be blinded by the dark,
but my cloudy breath sits in the cold, stays
a while, floats away. immolate, to mummify.
throw in a couple of mirrors for memory.
no one else is watching. my heat drifts right
on by, in the smoking remains that reclaim
my own reflection.

Flesh and Bones

i am stretched taut like a tightrope. i wait
for you, right ear close to the ground, until
i feel the weight of your body on my spine,
one foot at the back of my neck, pressing
for an answer. you make a firm claim, say.
you kneel down, dig dull nails into my shell,
make me pliable and understanding, yes.
my skin, uncharted grenadine. my hair,
hushed wilderness on the floor. pureness
and stance, ceremonial silence, on hold
as i order the body to remember to forget.
you disappear into my mane like a tangled
snake on a riverbank, and when you pull
at my locks one strand at a time, you steer
me right back to where you take me, wide
awake.

Stonewalling

am i talking to a wall? is the wall cracked,
covered in chipped paint, a dull, shifty gaze,
irregular indents? has it been standing there
a while, waiting, aging? is the wall a shade
of grey or blue, or grey-blue, crowded clouds
before mid-week summer rain? if i look closer,
can i spot faint fingerprints left behind
on the fractures? who left them? why would
the wall not tell me? does it not remember
how they got there? why would the wall
refuse to say, knowing it has ears if not eyes,
and that it never forgot a single word i said?

The Marshmallow Experiment

the body isn't strange. connect two bodies. learn
to understand one with another. speak of truth

with the corporeal. flash forward to your senses.
mediate flesh with blood. meditate with time. resist

the impulse to take what is right in front of you.
here's to hoping for more. pick up the intangible

with mental shortcuts. graze with an avid gaze.
devour with mousy bites. we are exquisitely satiated

when hunger peaks. & there's a bored god supposedly
recognizing our poise. but what if we don't like

sweet cushioned falls. what if gelatin is *haram.*
would we still be rewarded for holding out?

Stand Up Straight

you could smile, emphasis on possibly, though
it's hard to do so without hiking your shoulders
up. you slide undetected, perfecting the outline
of inhibition well—ears converging with trapezius,
aw, shucks-style, with a dash of compulsory
meekness. you learned the posture young,
an imprint on your nape. now you hope to stretch
your neck by pulling on the skin of a dusty photo
from 1989. the paper bends, you lean out of
yourself, wondering what sign the moon is in
that it vexes you to be alive with dust and dead
skin cells littering the floor. you pinch the throat,
you are five times the child you once were,
extending the space between crown and tail,
until the photo rips.

A Crack in Everything

my feet drag me here, to this abandoned lot. again,
a need for light among lowhung clouds, a long pole
poking the skies. i see it happen: my feet stepping
over faded lines, arbitrary borders, filling the hollow
between my toes with flowerless weeds. how they
persist through cracks. cohen would call them light.
looking to the bright yellow shell sheltering me
from gorged skies, i trudge toward soot-stained
walls, the promise of a sign. the cost to dream is
crabgrass stems pasted on my heels. in every blade,
the ability to live—lush forests covering concrete,
filling empty rooms, breathing in new life with
rain that bursts at last, cutting thick air in stride,
growing the softest meadow to cushion my feet.

The Cause of Sleepwalking Is Unknown

i suppose i would be frightened if i were my mother stumbling upon me, her daughter, rocking herself on her grandmother's rocking chair in the dim basement, soft light wood underneath small hands hovering.

what are you doing there, child, tucked in the lap of a pine womb?

it is unclear whether the creaking against the floor in the dead of night woke my mother, or whether she intuited it.

i climbed the gently curved structure, glassy-eyed, filled the absence, shifted my weight until i found the plumb line.

a cradling chair with arms, legs, and a back.

a wooden body enfolding another, smaller body.

the seat of all things.

years later, when i ask my mother what she remembers, she tells me of another story, how i used to wake up terror-stricken, "baba is burning."

memory is sleeping, sleeping memory, walking away from a father in flames.

memory is shifting, rebuilding a house reduced to ashes.

how we are seated in life, in the lotus of the heart.

Handiwork

my mother's nails are never long. always cut
short, no chance to form, a habit from growing
up on a farm. i have never seen lacquer, scarlet,
fine fingers sweeping notes. but i have seen
blue—tributaries and veins on achromatic skin,
blood-flooded riverbeds. when she knits, stitches,
embroiders, sows and mends, her hands grow
ochre sunrises and tangerine dreams slick with
reckoning. her hands sink into the well-draining
soil of her garden in the mountains and pull out
self-permission. again and again, i ask how can
such ragged care create such delicate things?
there are no words to the song, she says,
you just gotta sing.

The Great Escape

i am a fugitive, a runaway. my only crime
an extraction of the self. though running is
a stretch—i barely catch my breath. instead,
i walk. a slow, careful stride. i put on three
layers of winter coats in the middle of a hot
august night, tiptoe down the stairs past my
half-sleeping brother while my father conducts
important business in the bathroom. an anomaly
in his nighttime routine, the currents churning.
i leave a note on the bed, typed and printed
en anglais, for him to read in the morning.
or rather, for someone else to read for him
in the morning. my father struggles with words,
and despite our shared blood we rarely speak
the same language. now i flee and i bleed
another blood. by dawn, there is no fajr prayer,
no body. i take mine with me, dawn at my feet.
i leave a scene sticky with absence: my bed
and its ink-stained yorgan, my sad grandmother,
our sunday morning pancakes. of the few things
my father embraced from this country, maple
syrup was undoubtedly the sweetest.

After Breakfast

after Elin Danielson-Gambogi

the steeliest of bluesy teal,
a sigh of smoke that spills
no tea. there is sugar on my
cigarette mouth. bellis perennis,
because i won't say lackadaisical
daisies. the shell of youth over
slouched eggshell arms, pink
cheeks, sour bread. don't knock
on wood for me. i won't hold
my breath.

II.

To Rewrite Memory

the extraordinary capacity of the human mind
to rewrite memory is in the way i forget blood

    cycles with the moon in cast iron tubs. mind
    you, blood bathwater circles sweetest on skin

that recounts the days, old tales of shedding skin.
whether we remember a particular event at all

    is a matter of warmth. how burning or not at all
    must water be to scald the self of memory?

blood a clock that serves me right, memory
boiling by my moon design. most day-to-day

    experiences pass into oblivion, and a day
    knows its way to midnight. if only it was only

time, a seedless hourglass exceeded—no, only
the extraordinary capacity of the human mind.

The Wounded Deer

after Frida Kahlo

i didn’t think i would find you
in this deep messy forest, serpent
eyes on my dearest antlers, shooting
arrows at my mottled armour.
you weren’t always so fond
of blood blooms, now you hunted
the marks on my soaked coat,
pleased with yourself as i skittered
like bambi in the sunless rainwater
that pooled at the foot of selfsame
trees. i took to the glass of the ocean,
mirrored hope of blue, and the sibilant
sky never asking for it. i didn’t either,
and leapt away.

A Blue So Deep

i let you know i am not ready
for this kind of royalty. a blue
so deep you take a sickle
to my hand and draw it in—
the surrender like a shard.
i am neither ready nor used
to it. your mouth on my neck
a means to an end, to go
elsewhere. somewhere else,
as in, speaking of the pulse.
in a body that needs less
turbulence, i look up to her
all the time. the moon and
her iridescent grief braided
in my tresses. i sit back, sip
black molasses from a cup
more turmeric than milk, not
to be the cost. i was pregnant
with a timepiece once, chose
to extract the cornflower seeds,
scoop them all out—far, so far
from myself i was beside myself.

Clara: Ecstasy

we are curious about anatomy, most notably our own.

we have similar bodies, though not quite the same, and we often wonder why a dress falls a certain way on one but not the other.

between us, we know four languages.

one of us excels in one more than the other.

the other masters one the other can only read.

and sometimes, as one of us dives deeper into a jargon, the other slowly drifts away from it.

on a red linen tablecloth, she writes the arabic word for love in chalk.

and in a room full of turks, she asks:

"mutlu musun?"

but i can't answer because i don't know what happy means.

we love alphabet soup, our idea of exhilaration.

sitting before full-length mirrors, letters into our mouths, we often compare forms until we are only left with our tongues.

Panacea

if i could breathe five mississippis / if i could turn my tongue seven thousand times / before sneaking / before suspicions / if i could bow my head to my knees and sigh between my thighs / if i could sway with petty fated leaves instead of hanging onto their stems / for dear life / if i could hug the bush, the thorns / if i could harvest rosehip and marjoram / if in the hollow of my waist i could loosen you up / unravel your grip / if i could stiffen to soften / if i could twist the spindle of your spine to straighten mine / if i could grow spring inside the jet-black torrent of my dead dark hair / if i could, i would / drink it up, if i could / drink it all, and look / beyond the realm of possibility / look / sometimes it's the only way / to call it / relief

Scarecrow

my chest stuffed with fine chopped hay.
hey, you wouldn't know it, but i can be
scary sometimes. the way i'm always cold,
the nit-picking, my inability to have and
to hold. objections, winds idyllic—every-
thing passes right through my meshy parts.
my love unbecoming, i'd love to take flight,
but i've filled my entire body with hay.
hey, there is no food for these thoughts.
feed me with air and a murder of crows,
my wide shoulders for the crackling lungs
of black birds.

Index

flashbacks blink and blur

        in the afterglow of a late afternoon

freeze response. the trembling graphite,

        the lawless cursed

handwriting—my notes of carved lead,

        the depths of learned

helplessness,

hypersensitivity to threat.

        how much damage can one

immune system withstand? the leaves on

        a philodendron, unlike this

inner void, are heart-shaped. the sun sets in

deep green veins, i look for it.

intimacy, as in difficult. intimacy as in

the answer to big stars dimming.

Clara: A Dinner

she brings half a bottle of white wallaroo trail wine.

i cook colours, beige upon beige, set them up in a circle with a dot of nothing in the middle.

she tries on my value village astrakhan winter coat and it fits her like a glove.

i put on my red robe.

white wallaroo trail wine moves in between two bodies dressed.

i send a message that lies in limbo.

she does the same.

i pour leftover huntley vineyard wine from a bottle that hasn't yet been added to the row of empties on the counter.

we conclude that wallaroo trails are better than monkey trails because wallaroos are considerably nicer than monkeys.

we layer up and walk to the dépanneur across the 51 stop.

we buy dessert—chocolate chip cookies, an oh henry candy bar, another bottle.

we eat the chocolate, we drink the wine.

i burn three sticks of stale amber incense with a side of tobacco and tar.

we forget that the purpose of our meeting was for us to go shoot a video with a foot fetishist.

the foot fetishist calls us to inform us that it is over.

i drop resting soil all over the kitchen counter and in my study.

a cat knocks over a glass and it shatters into a million pieces.

at the end of the night, she says:

"remember when we went to the dépanneur?"

and i do, smiling at how long ago it had been.

Foreshadowing

after Francesca Woodman

the watery wallpaper, the chipped paint
on the slope of her neck. her soft stomach
of pensive asymmetry, how she covered
her naked back with dilapidation, hand
in a fist. consider the vermillion between
her thighs, her wish for the pull of mud
in that moment, idling. she finds it in
the walls, blending with the missing
windows, the shards under her splinter-
covered feet, paving the way down under.

Nightstand, or How to Clear Your Aura

eyelashes plucked
an empty perfume bottle
never full echo half-
broken bowl glued up
a veil or prayer or
moonlight dust soil
dry mirror framed
gold tissue
paper notes, books
a comb, hair discarded
dolls' eyes
a basket of dried dandelions
kodak instamatic
black gloves with holes
hollowed out ceramic pigeon
gut-filled with sea things
coral and one loose screw
scrap of bark
words from the trees
crows of ink and metal
coin purse with coins

from other places
where-been when-left
triangle of water
pointed humidity
time a selenite wand

Daylight Savings Time Ends

watch me as i burrow in a chest of snow, cheeks burnt
from the chill. i am learning to be with the seasons, even

the cold ones. see through me and the bloodless bank,
white on white, a splintering sheath. the sun sets so early

it might as well be late. i kiss my lips with one finger.
shhh—my phone rings, the rumble of wings, a partridge

takes flight. did you hear that? yes, i saw ground-
grazing feathers, my cold gloved hands cupping one hour

of lost light, the waxing gibbous rising unpresumptuous,
air unbothered by city excess, a silvery rabbit on my solar

plexus. you tuck the balled up beast between my breasts,
hear my crackling footsteps on frozen leaves, trailing spoor

to the dusk song of watchful birches. i smear my wintering
body in earnest with furless hands. i understand to seize

this chance on my chest, cottontail luck to weather winter.

Time Out

it is not the sun i see dormant under lock and key,
light flitting in and out of a slit below the door.
it is not the sun, but a milling morning. dust
of borrowed bread. i confess: there is not much
to say when my jaw is this clenched. my tongue
loosens, covers miles upon miles of sunburnt
range, but it cannot follow the single red thread
of rage back to my mouth. i wish i could say,
i am angry. i am upset at my bones, how brittle
they've become in the sinkhole of my back.
i wish i could throw the tantrum, arms flailing,
and throw it away. instead, i pull a star out of
the wild wheat blades and imagine it like a pardon.
i let it burn smokeless behind the wooden divide
while my glowing lungs exhale a fossil.

Is That a Silver Lining?

the second day of january, a sunday with no light.

i get a call.

a voice instead of a recording, truth instead of deceit.

who answers the phone anymore?

i pick up for a bored man saying the doctor wants to see me.

new year, old news, acquiescence, settling on a date.

i wait for hours in a room poorly designed for waiting.

plastic everything, humour lost on the best of us.

the doctor calls me by my second name.

who am i if i don't recognize myself?

a mask holds my face in place. fate, and tension in the jaw.

fabric does little for breath.

he uses words like “severe” and “alarming.”

my bones are old, i am young.

“did i make you cry?”

sure, but the nurse says i have nice eyes.

Tell Me What You Know About Dismemberment

after Bhanu Kapil

if the universe is a whole, and i am you
and you are i, then we are everyone, and
a lack of belonging is missing limbs.
it is a severing of the self from a crowd
of strangers, blood family, or friends.
the disquieted running on empty. i am
someone's lost arm, the world's one skin
cell, and the idea of not relying on other
people to make my own decisions is still
a frightening mystery. it is not what am i
missing, but whom am i missing? every-
one and everything. i am missing myself,
missing my thinly disguised self.

Some Call It Magic

he gestures toward the vinyl-tired room, a feather
on the floor. he waits while i undress and lie on
the table, knocks gently on the door. to understand
my body, he looks at me in the eyes. sclera before
fascia. a space heater whirs without a shiver.
imagine a beginning, a wool string wrapped around
a goldenrod neck. light disappearing. closed eyes
moving energy and masses. one hand between
my legs, under my sacrum, the other on my wing
of ilium. i study the drop-down ceiling, count dots
in beige polystyrene. i want to straighten a lifted
square, wish he could shift my bad back. he tells me
to stop talking, by which he means my eyes. i look
to listen to the pinching inside my left thigh, how
it points to a wreath of barbs. i wear this crown.
afterward, i stand behind his desk, dressed. he shows
me how to write my name in ge'ez. he writes me
a part of him. i scratch my scalp, no blood.

Below the Waist

i wish i could say i didn't feel the clockwork windstorm
closing in around my sacrum. every day, barbed stems

of bright red ligaments legitimately cling to my wings,
bone to bone. this is a climate issue, a local one, starting

at the root. i've been sitting too long. i talk about it often,
how my back holds on to contraction, binding old,

inflammatory stories to this low-blow place. this is about
a shielded body. this is about prickly petals sweeping up

swarms of memories that dared prevail in connective tissue.
it knows the score i did not think to keep. but watch even

as known thunder hits me, even as wails of rain drain me,
that strained hunger for a moment of relief finds peace,

somehow, in a blazing band of garnet roses.

U R Güzelyou; I U Seviyorme

a goose drenched in oil

yes, please, and—

an axis in a play of light

unleashing the unnecessary

honest hour overlooking the trail

unfathomed slants, twists and edges

the whispered-spoken sound of your voice

a mystifying waltzing on air

dancing by the shore

the heat in your hand

braiding my hair

the all-knowing eyes and their calligraphy

imprints that time knows how to erase

or engrave

a dark bird

Clara: A Gemini Moon

your shoulders of milk quilted in daffodil, your tattered eva b cardigan. how you amble toward me in your stiff betty page haircut as i leave the club, lashes and nose full of snow. pocket phones do not exist, much like my belief in any ability to console—but you know better. we are still timid. stranger sisters, outsiders in love with one another. i hold your hand, your teeth-ravaged nails. i walk your porcelain shiver into the marbled winter. how cold you are, a monday night kind of frozen, bleeding a life you did not know you carried. i sit you catatonic in my black velvet armchair. you and i, we will cross the strait many times in search of a clouded moon, eyes gauzy with urgency.

Heart Gallery

i weave my hands in a garland of twigs
and bones. my heart in the heart of it. there,
where trees hum, cheer me to lift it all and
let it fall like sand, every bit of skeleton
a key to an old address, what feels like home
but isn't, what feels like hope but more
of a thump, ink in my palms, notes to self.
there is time there, things i've done, colours
and wood, my own map. yesterday i wondered
where i was, looked no closer to the fingers
laced on my chest, soaking sweat, all this
blood running wild.

III.

The Illuminated Heights of an Empty Candy Jar

i want to melt into all the sand
flowers and their leafless stems,
dried sprigs
and gold-plated chains, at night
i take off my heavy rings.
i give myself barren containers
fill them up
fill them with marble balls from pamukkale,
bronze moons, evil eyes,
fill them with copper arrows
and dried up liquor from years
of quitting drinking.
i want their patterns to clash, arabesques
on a beige wall
cast from a crystal tip, the sacred
geometry of dust-covered glass
a clear light cave.

My Grandfather Was a Kurdish Alevi from Erzincan

my grandfather was a kurdish alevi from erzincan.

i remember this an ocean's throw from his burial plot below the taurus mountains, over a meal of tuna pot pie, buttered corn on the cob and diced tomato salad prepared by my mother.

my grandfather had a severe nose and a weak chin and when he smiled with thick parentheses around his mouth, i wondered if his face hurt.

he worked in the mines and drank tea dark as soot. on eid, he lined up sheep skulls and entrails on stone walls around the bleached shrubbed yard. thick blood pooled around the fences, flies buzzed, stray calico cats named pico and piccolo yearned for a loot of discarded innards.

a wide-eyed child, i examined the horns sliced out of their heads, beauty in sacrificial artifice, murderer mementos.

i didn't kill the sheep, but unsparing hands served me their boiled tripe in an opaline puddle of lemony milk sprinkled with red pepper flakes.

my grandfather was a dede, my father is a dede, my father's chin isn't weak but he has a broken nose and burnt skin. we call these men dede and we fear them because we do not know them and their smiles so quickly vanish when one of us laughs too hard or leaves a hair in the sink.

Spoon

i wasn't born with a silver spoon in my mouth, but my grandmother gave me a crystal sugar bowl that paints rainbows across the wall, and above it hangs a spoon of stainless chromium plate, the next best thing. i've picked sugar with it, stirred drinks, swallowed medicine, measured spices, broken eggshells, cut melted wax, retrieved earrings from a drain, pressed it against my uvula and expelled long, wasted nights. it held sugar, dusty petals. inside, a miniature universe, an ocean, the surface of the world reflected in heat. i cup the spoon against my ear and listen to the whispers of elsewhere, elsewhere beckoning.

Tulips at Night

perennials everywhere. i steal a tulip
on my way home from karaköy.
in a rakı-infused dream i make it mine,
plucked from the soil where it mingled
freely with her sisters. a swift & selfish
kidnapping, an impulse in the night.
i give the flower a new home in the curves
of a tea glass. on a book she blooms,
never minding that it is past midnight.
in the morning, she greets me with coral
lines and a sly smile. i don't know what
she makes of her new sights, but i left
a world too, so we can learn together.

Clara: Glossary

i am drinking cold tea.

made it earlier today.

by the time i could drink it, i had to leave the pot behind on my desk, untouched.

i went to the mouth of *istiklal* ("independence"), the busiest pedestrian street of *beyoğlu* ("son of a lord"), for a small cocktail event dedicated to a hollywood actor of swedish descent known for his height and fangs.

i did not meet him. instead, i spoke to his childhood friend about things both of us have already forgotten.

a plate of stuffed vine leaves floated our way.

"*dolma* means filled," i said.

there was an agreeable nod somewhere.

i left.

the *tünel* ("underground funicular") led me to the dock, but i missed the *vapur* ("ferry") by a minute. i waited twenty more for the next.

in the window reflection, a man played the *kemençe* ("small bow").

outside, the sea, black, and the white trail of the wake.

inside, fellow passengers all eager to reach the other side.

a long day for many of them. for me, too.

you know all these words, clara.

you let me have them with cold tea.

Apartment Six

the glow-in-the-dark stars pasted on the bedroom
ceiling never light up to a crystal jellyfish blue-green

sheen, but when my upstairs neighbour smokes
the hookah and bubble sounds make their way down

the paper-thin walls, i am in a foggy aquarium.
to blend with the waters, to shoo away wandering

mouths, jellyfish light up their bell-shaped bodies
in a disco party though there is nothing to celebrate—

dancing is the escape. my neighbour is not a sea
anemone with stinging tentacles, he is every man

blowing smoke, and i yearn for an invisibility
cloak, skin to ceiling, stars as my witness.

Multiple Mirrors

after Patricia Renée Ewing

multiple mirrors carry heavy reflection,
unburdened. every part of your body chop-
ped up in a disappearing act. bouquet
the pieces, tie them with a double-knotted
bow. you are rich in the way that you imagine
yourself skipping like a dancer on stage with
bandaged feet, eyes winking at your fingertips.
lick every last jewel pasted on your neck like
it's the only thing worth your hunger.
because it is. you sliced yourself thin, bones
emptied of marrow. blew in a light so faint
through the myriad glass, you can't even see
the tumbling flesh spilling out of the frames,
ribbon undone.

Tongue Stories

story time: compliments on a red velvet case. the official asks, "are you sure you want to keep both names? it drags on the tongue." i am sure, i say. you would not remove a star from a soldier. think of a lone forbearing man under a black sky, opaque and unyielding; that is not a fair trade. the star and the soldier cannot be without one another.

story time: a window on a wall that leads to a hole. there is nothing in the hole, and the window has no pane. you cannot watch the sun rise from this room, but you can imagine the sun on your fingers. a song pulses and sneaks through the curtains, *here we are tongue-tied, before we collide*—and you narrowly miss it.

story time: around a table. all of our personalities compounded in our mother tongues, and all of our mother tongues wagging in various judgements of character. we are all in exodus, some form of it.

story time: when you press your finger on my lips, i swallow the silence and confine it to my chest. everyday i strive to pluck nightingales from my ribcage, hoping their melody pulls through and i find my tongue.

You Take My Portrait

there is only a difference in sequence between
sacred and scared. where do i sit: by the bosphorus,
by open books, at a marbled table, at the foot of
an unmade bed, on the edge of my seat, breath bated
or tied, ribbon-bound. where do i lie: on the tall green
grass, on a blush blanket, on the cat couch, on my back,
on the still water in a silence i cannot break for fear of
ruffling feathers, an idle spell. when you tell me to
shed it all, i know it's more than just a pluck. it is
an urge to remove all that gets in the way of the mind,
all that burdens the body from moving freely into the
world. by the window my head is a face, effaced,
becomes the reflection, the glass against the sky,
the glass against the sun, the glass against the leaves
of a tree that knows the rhythm of seasons in every bone.
in front of you i stand four-pointed, cardinal, star-naked
with the wealth of the world underneath my feet.
with a trick, a tilt and an angle, i am painted gold
by three eyes focused on a figure eight. as a seasoned
soul enclosed in skin and bark, i too bare all.

Fortune Cookie Argument

you move your arms unaware of muscle and tissue, the white noise of your body crackling heedless. you puff your chest of breath and faux-fury, and the light is black for you. the stars are already dead. a new headless moon rises and it cannot look you in the eyes. when you are done amassing ammunition for your next fortune cookie argument, come to me. i will take the bait, i will not bite. i will feed you agave nectar, plant the open sesame seed of your discontent, urge you to swallow. i will show you the last taste of your future. we will leave no paper trail. you are what you eat: lucky numbers, aphorisms, amorphous prophecies, my assent. you can turn in. double over. what is kept is a matter of taste. what is removed is a manner of speaking, noiseless.

Self-Portrait as Winter Bird

the honey locusts are bare. it's the weather, cast down
        like a flattened neck vein, a mouth full of seeds.

i was told i could not people-please my way into healing.

consider this half-decaf coffee: an indulgent compromise,
        indigestion in terry cloth, dim-lit consequences.

it's the weather, stubborn. let me return, it says,

but i am looking for some action, something to happen.
        there is gold in my abdomen, cinnamon sequins.

inflame me. i'm here for it. suffering for a small cup

of pleasure, not a thing of beauty. & do not barter, bird,
        i tell myself. you cannot trade your filler words.

your grand forevers, your molting wishes.

here is one: i would bring a best friend home. a best friend
        i would kiss on the mouth. i'm not trying

to keep warm. i'm going for the quill, beak wide open.

To Leave Again

she whirls, her mind in circles. she thinks the vertigo stems from the ferry rides shuttling her back and forth between shores. the boat sways. her compass wavers. even when she stands very still, her body moves between continents. the vertigo cannot be tamed, not with pills, not with ginger tea. the cold season settles, mist clings to the freezing waters of the strait. when hüzün and mutluluk come together in the rippling canvas of the water, they hesitate to commit. but no one has to choose. she doesn't, either. in-between is the only world she knows, and she carries it with her wherever she goes.

Better than a Fridge Magnet

i got stones, bright coloured jewels
from the sea. under brushing salt water,
you wouldn't think they'd turn grey as dust
as they dried, but we love the illusion,
the way a mouth opens: never wise, unable
to discern the taste it craves, a metallic urge
to speak in a language not yet mastered.
drop them like lozenges, the stones. my jaw
is a travertine terrace, and freedom is a leash
washed ashore, letting unusual candy melt
on the tongue. i define so that you understand
why it matters to me: how often we are muddled
against the implacable tide. how often we are
huddled against our own crashing waves,
toes mistaken for pebbles. i wanted magma,
i tried walking barefoot towards the fire,
i got these instead.

Back Alley Aubade

there are no two hands pressing wax together. you handed me this three-wick frankincense candle in lieu of a broken-down wooden fence. you counted on it to melt the ice-covered holes in the alley, lighten up the tired conifers sheltering an enclosure i can only glimpse from my first floor window. that's where i put it, on the edge, to remind me to take a look at what's out there. when i see the neighbour's backyard, i think of the dead magnolia, how they razed it, erased it for space. they're hard to come by, i hear. two weeks of pink blooms or a lifelong spot for a gas guzzler—the choice is clear. for me, anyway. but i don't own a yard, i have no rebellious trees pushing through tight pickets and the rusty spine of bicycles, fallen samaras scattered under snow. there are no two hands pressing wax together. frankincense's mysticism escapes me, too frank and i'm incensed, craving oudh, mirrored windows and haunting leaves for all this foam and garbage under the balcony.

More Cold Tea

i stub my toe on the closet door
curl and cuss arrested
in breath
i press fingers
pull skin
seal eyes shut
how can i move
from velvet gowns
to the edge of the bed
without a yelp
or help
my lives flash me by
all one of them
multitudes
i haven't earned them
in this bedroom
i only notice the bottom
of my dresses
black on black on black beguiling
i admit i am easily
foretold
at least i haven't burned
the door down
i haven't acquiesced to

the ire of hangers
and i can still tell apart
spilled milk from
anger pain
from cold tea

Private Property

winter still and i do not understand
how time ambles on as if it cannot pause
long enough to take in the snow angels
we stamped on this frozen lake. melting
flakes tucked up our sleeves like fleeting
tricks, we have not talked for three days.
i am not sulking in my heavy boots, but
underneath us, the ice expands and cracks,
and i worry about falling in, though sinking
with a body that cannot fold seems unlikely.
side by side in silence, i swindle my voice
into softness. i fondle the horizon for an ivory
sun and your forgiveness. the only sign before
me is toppled, *propriété privée*, a sad puppet
with winged arms searching for wide heavens
it cannot reach. i get it. you just need a little
more time before you can grant me back
access to your tender parts.

Scarification

i only needed a minute to heat up a dime with flame
and fury, place it on my arm with the sole purpose of

reigniting the sun. in time, it became a moon with two
birthmark stars, or a happy accident in a deliberate act.

six years in, it still itches, as if to say: do not forget.
here is me remembering: wounds heal in stages, slip

through crust, mantle and outer core until reduced
to intense heat in the innermost part of our bodies.

at the age of six, a child starts to grasp time, develops
the ability to manipulate sounds, to know the difference

between same and different. in the rumpled skin of my
arm, the moon is the sun, which is all the same to me.

Breastbone

the world rises in and out of the mouth of babes
and i cannot tell my weak teeth from the still life
etched between my breasts. i am drawn to it,
so much raw that if i were to take an unlucky shot
in the dark, i would line up and stack all my foiled
coins for a win. i shoot this instead—rusty arrows
skyward, sleeves full of goosebumps posing as
misdirection—and i ask, where are you, sun?
where have they wrapped you up and hidden you?
i open petals on my nightfield, but none have
your vision. i rise off-white covered in a sheeted
wing ghost wheels turning by the shadow of
moonchild-me and a star out like a light i cannot
see. there is somewhere for all of us. the bright-
est went to dream dans le firmament. maman,
je n'ai pas tant dormi. i got lost along the way,
but tucked in my busted slope, i found the sun
this light a moon and me a child.

Apology Accepted

you were wrong to tweak the branch
between your fingers, bereft little thing.
you were wrong to snap, brittle twig
dead or dying. you were right over
the line, but she heard you say sorry.
on your knees you cowered enough.
shit happens. look at the wind, how
it never stops rolling out a red carpet for
single-winged whirlybirds that warn us
of seasons, show us where to ground
our feet. your eyes imagine countless
worlds in search of spun sugar, something
lukewarm and familiar, the overripe sun,
the harried rain. but when your arms fold
over the breath of maples that have known
sweetness, there is no room for rigidity.
see under which tree your toes land.
see how you are welcomed home.

Some Kind of Light

the first morning of spring, it isn't, but it gives us a taste.

the plants are thirsty, stems languid. i mist them with vinegar by mistake. i wipe their leaves one by one, strokes long and generous. i could be swimming,

but i am bleeding scales.

my voice a muscle that gleans in and out of range.

i squeeze half a lemon into a glass of water and it spills in a ray of light on the counter.

in spring we cannot believe our eyes at the sun.

our blood coursing for another season to seize, for another season to cease.

clara, you are stroking your mother-in-law's mottled skin.

your name—a shining light. a golden akhal-teke mare in the northeasternmost state, ushering the way.

her body is curled into a transient bed in the living room, the one you say your goodbyes in. there's a rug underneath it. a magic kilim or a life raft, keeping her afloat.

in spring the water knows of us melting.

eau de rêve, you are dreamed about cascading and clear.

she lies under a gilded winter landscape, a figure sliding down a hill, a trail of two lines, mist on the penobscot river, the snow not yet thawing.

clara, you are holding her hand when she whispers, "let me die."

i cannot hold water between my own palms. even tears plan their escape from the corner of my eyes, around the bones.

we make our own rivers.

at night, i rub rosehip oil on my face. deep orange, liquid gold, and i wonder which two lines i am anointing.

drowning never occurs to us in dreams.

clara, you are there when she pulls at her skin and says, "let me out of here."

so much of this skin holding. holding blood, holding kin.

her fever covered in a quilt.

blood warming underneath the patchwork.

it isn't so much chaos as it is pieces coming together, calling you daughter.

the white light and frigid weather in a mouth cheating for spring.

the lemon water, still, leaving a halo of the morning.

IV.

Tempting Fortune for a New Dawn

seven days before my birthday, my partner announces a need for time and space.

it isn't so much a declaration as it is a whisper, crestfallen and withered, blue eyes turning grey.

still, i spend two days exhausting my lachrymal reserves.

clara, you are pregnant. 11 weeks, on the cusp of the point of no return.

i love them—the fruit inside your body.

11 weeks, though by now it might be 12. men around you have opinions. an abortion, cutting out the father.

but we daughters know better.

on the eve of my birthday, my partner and i take a break from our break to convene among tall red pines.

we are good at pausing, resuming.

i say goodbye to a decade and welcome another, washing breakfast dishes in the shower, squatting on polished stones with unconcerned spiders. bits of scrambled eggs and coffee grounds swirl by my feet and are swallowed by the drain.

clara, here's the truth as i swim in murky waters: we double our lives, and you are already taking care of the fig-plum better than anybody ever will.

my partner lies next to me, rubs my back. hand an abstraction, circles on the skin, immaterial like time, though sometimes i catch a feeling in grey-blue eyes, a sliver of sky.

it could be the bullfrog song, or

the water lilies dotting the horizon—

but in the evening, we play music, and i howl like a wolf.

Crab Love

i was born from a wound

my muslin muslim heart at the cross

of a headless saint sur le grand chemin de la haute-folie

thank you for remembering i was born with the dawn

maman de la chute with only future in palms

6:06 a.m. cancer sun promise of another life

thank you for birthing me in this city of all cities

with a single long breath, who knows what came first

in that heavy wind—the sigh or the cry & following

my hurried exit from hospitable womb to hospital room

thank you for holding me in your arms

claws slight and supple grasping around your finger

not cutting in this mouth, there are only fragments

maman made mine or me

long hair hers light mine dark coiling into an early spring

the red of our blood cannot show through such thick skin

i have dreams to fulfill

yours too

i will never birth a child with the sun rising in my palm

but i have callouses on my feet and i know how to dance

The Great Divide

i move through the cloud forest, pull up my shirt.
bear with me as i bare my breasts for trees
veiled in soft moss and lichen, for shy bellbirds.
i stand on two continents, hidden from view,
chest agape, seafoam steam rising. i didn't always
show this much skin. skin the colour of piss,
my brother used to say. between east and west,
i won the husk of difference. hide my skin,
heed barked orders, that's what i learned to do.
but here in the mountain range, a brave sunray
peeks through the hazy cover, passes jade leaves
and settles in the undergrowth. i am hot, you see,
covered in coins, humid with expectation and desire
to photosynthesize. i turn to you, my canopy trees
shrouded in mist, my furtive wattled birds. i say
who knew piss was just another word for gold.

Holding On to Let Go

i take a long look at the cotoneaster shrubs
lining the street between my home
and the office of a man who once left
a cluster of flaming marks on my back.
as the first flush of morning clings
onto their ovate leaves, my sight
switches to thirst. i pick a sprig of red berries,
pluck a few, bottle them like fireflies.
i want to leave the jar at his door,
but there are orange cones everywhere,
a sign that reads *trottoir barré.*
it's hard to catch the cloudless eternity
of a moment, yet there is one: berries ripe
for appetite, ambition to be consumed.

Kismet

light rain is heavy when it drops on parched earth.
a stranger asks a question for which they already
know the answer. i see through the guise,
but i answer anyway. i was raised to be polite.
i could have been a mother by now, but i am not.
i am not dewy cotton on which to fall. not a bundle
of reason parading comfort for the lost. i am modest
velvet, scuffed black boots. with any luck i shine
them into presence, a verse in a vision, brighter eyes.
when the stranger tells me, you will be one soon,
i think of poppy seeds, the foot of a tree, the hurt
that sits between us. we react from a place of knowing.
i let the stranger have certitude for a thing that hangs
by a split-end, unaware it has already been buried.

Île-Aux-Tourtes Bridge Partially Reopened Friday Morning, Additional Lane Opens Monday

metro doors are heavy and no one wants to touch them.

i slide outside like a sheet, sit on a slab of concrete and watch cars line up for food that's fastly served, food to be balanced on laps, food for the carousel joyride, the merry go 'round and 'round and 'round we go.

an old brown man sits next to me, drinks his canadian coffee. i wait. he's company.

in my phone, a cackle of women squeal about meat and men while my partner's partner reminds me of who i will never be.

i look at the brown man, i look at my phone. the city is an island.

i do not notice my brother in the parking lot with his crowning vehicle, sporting utility. if i need to empty my body, now's the time, he says, but i have no need for the thrones of alleged burger kings.

in the backseat, a handful of a boy wakes up from a nap, eyes blinking.

"are you feeling better?"

my nephew smiles and i think, how nice to be asked.

my brother complains about my mother, my father. i, too, ease into the banter, though i wonder if there are other ways we can relate to one another.

my nephew points out train tracks, a yellow crane, a siberian husky popping through a sunroof.

how are you, we cannot ask, only whisper, breathe out, hide between other words.

how are you, as an idle act, elusive between the lips of those with whom i share blood.

at the house, my niece stands on the porch beaming, surrounded by a cackle of little women squealing, no meat nor men in sight.

“c’est ma tante,” she declares, as i kneel to squeeze her in these arms that have never lived but to hold.

we have crossed the river somehow, we have made it here.

in the evening, my brother drives me to the train station. tracks are safer to follow than broken bridges.

through the window, i point things out to myself: wagons, houses, graffiti. stops with names like cedar park and pine beach.

the city is an island, i know.

i had to leave it to make it home.

Containment List

the silvery mesh ball ringing on the side of a saffron diamond cup.

my heavy late-night hair falling on my shoulders, how it absorbed the tangy sweat of your arched, flushed forehead like a sea sponge. you said it smelled of rosemary, mermaid tricks.

mild stinging nettle tea on pursed lips, how i ran my tongue on loose leaves that escaped the strainer as if to remember them, a habit i forgot i picked up from my father.

my father's white diesel truck pulling into the driveway, my wide-eyed gasp and sprint up the interminable stairs, how i closed the postered bedroom door shut, held my breath.

that single piece of damp, mouldy maple bark i retrieved from under decaying leaves on the washed-out mid-november mountain.

the vintage 1970s mint green futon i purchased for fifty dollars at an estate sale in outremont, how the springs creaked and the left side dipped more than the right. i couldn't sit on it without thinking about a dead man who sat there for hours watching the news and reading the news until he became the news.

Tango Injuries

it's been hard to get me out of the house these days
with these old habits dying hard. it helps if i prep
everything in advance: soft high heels, forgettable
dress, toothbrush. i battle discomfort for a dance,
climb the stairs of dingy buildings, chase bandoneon
notes with ears perked like a cat—this, my one wild
and precious life. oh mary, have you ever pranced
around a room hoping for a glance? tango starts
with the eyes, you see. i keep that contact intact,
follow the nod, the gracious hand on my back.
i forgive wavering stances, wandering nails sifting
through my bare skin. and in the morning, i survey
the evening. deep blue, chartreuse, purple-red.
a rare night-blooming cereus captured at the crack
of dawn. invisible ink imprints revealed by the sun.
so many answered prayers, the evidence of bodies.

Clara: The Fruit Aisle

the hazel in your iris, two wings of ink
on the outskirts of your universe, stars
made of pupils. you lean on your son
in the squealing cart by the papayas,
the bananas, the pears, the thick caramel
sauce that you never considered buying.
the smell of your baby's apricot cheeks.
your eyes two brass lamps, freckles in
a pink punch skyline.

Love's Secret Domain

here is the miracle: sparrows,
flapping wings, eagerness to cut
through the wind.
i listen to a coil song and coil
on the ground, drawing infinity
with one foot. i think about
the underwatered severed world,
but here i am looking at the sky
to explain the mad love rose
that sprouted inside and made
my arms efflorescences aching
for flight. who is to say
where the spinning comes from,
only that somewhere from above
it connects itself to the earth.
and in an effort to stand taller,
i pinch my ankle
the hint of a sting
my bottom line.

Metamour

for Son

my eyes in my stomach flickering, but no appetite

your smile is kind and i could never doubt it

your hand in my hand, we hold the same body

i am you, you are i, and in between us is a shared love

for another us, the same human, and an angel that sings

what's so wrong with the light?

at the table, under a blanket, we are fed pieces of enoki

slender fingers entwined like stems, our bodies cold

we cradle the same heart, my shoulder, your neck

and our thickening thoughts

in the layers of a watchful fire from another corner

i learn so much about you, my not-a-junkie

you are in tune with all manners of living

et j'ai vu l'oiseau rouge rising

as it entered my ear, slid behind my eyes, flit along my throat

we don't say it enough, i am glad you exist

but we are holding these very words right here

in our split bodies made whole

Self-Care as Demolition

the walls are moving. tumbling walls falling.
i undo the home. i break the skeleton, the back-
bone. foundation alone could move mountains.
i shake it up. take it apart. kiss a side, turn it
inside out. plop it face down on the ground.
lie on it. give it warmth. i loosen the screws
of every single piece of furniture i ever owned.
teak table, chairs. oak trees chiseled in drawers
stuffed with pale pink things. i pile up wood
and spunk, can't say i would know where to find
fuel. i tug at blackout curtains, rip a piece of lace
from the edge of the soaked hot night, stuff it
in my mouth, sing, sing my voice to a full-stop.

If a Name Falls in a Forest

i haven't said your name in so long.

though i remember how it sounds—
an unfurling of letters,
two syllables, prayer beads
on the tongue, sacred and suited.

your name cuts through the air,
leaves a trail in the curtain winds.

when i waved goodbye, i mouthed it
in the back of my hand,

yes, i said,
and your name in the same breath.

Smokeless Djinn

everyone is gone, gone-ing. not that i could
have built us a picket fence in this free rein
of a space. we dreamt more than we shaped
our perfect queer life, mashallahs plentiful.
i wanted to give you my mother, my father—
our knotty love. i wanted to fill your orphaned
heart with more than a steady influx of words.
but we talked too much until it was too little,
and we ran out of life to live with one another.
now i walk backwards to the silver break
in the clouds, before my wilful infertility,
before your slow fade. shadows coat the sky
like my mother's brown & black wool shawl.
you loved those colours too—the lack of them.
cold comfort to bury yourself in, die a bit.

Ampersands

i don't understand why bodies are exposed,
my brother says, unwilling to enter the funeral
home. & i want to tell him that when a flame
stops burning, smoke rises & disappears.
this is just a small way for us to hold the smoke
between our palms. we keep the cloud close to
home & remember life in a body emptied of it,
this great vessel of undoing. my brother does not
want to go in, but i tell him i can go with him,
stand by the glossy casket to hide the remains,
make trite conversation about family traditions
even though he is angry at me. i chose silence
for a while, but not for years. & we are standing
together, are we not? there is *again*, embodied.
& there is still movement as we tilt forward,
one step in front of another. we make our way
through the hot stuffy room, my back shielding
cold skin, & it's no big deal. we are all living
& dying. & i am willing to hold the cloud
for the two of us.

On Belonging

my mother thought fresh figs were strange,
full of worms. refused to eat them without
stubborn theatrics. i admired her conviction,
but i loved figs, how they dissolved between
my fingers into a velvet pulp. she melted too,
once, after meeting my father in a sailors bar.
so much so that she flew to his village by the
turquoise coast where, lips bone-dry, drank
a too-warm ayran. she hated it and was sick,
still to this day can't fathom how anyone can
touch it, but i love the tang of yogurt and salt.
i crave it with pickles and a gulp of şalgam,
why not, because the only way to eat turnips
is to drink them. my mother knew how to feed
her child. and my mother knew how to feed
herself so that her child of two worlds could
remember the nuance.

The Inn of the Dawn Horse

after Leonora Carrington

beyond the morningtide curtains,
my fleeting white horse flies through
spartan junipers. so long with the dawn,
pale beast, but i kept an effigy of you
in the back of my mind, a reminder
of my youngling years for every unknown
tomorrow. i listen to my shadow now,
some call it work, and uncover at my
fingertip all that was erased. blotted-out
memories brew hidden on the ground,
while my medusa hair floats away,
calling for perseus.

Where Now?

first, an idea of thorns, even in the absence of colour.

we know the sting, but when bougainvilleas rise on innocent walls to cover them, inch by inch, no matter the way, we always come back to pink bracts, and their assumed softness.

i am trying to say what we already know: that the bite hurts more than the teeth. that in seething there is a song, or hot water for tea.

we are not afraid to bleed out every seven years.

my home is under full sunlight, in the heart of palm-sized cotton candy nests waiting for bees, and i am a beast pollinated by pointed edges, sharp fangs disarmed by presence.

the subtext: does this closure make me look open enough?

perhaps i am also tolerant of drought.

i have not forgotten about the importance of regular pruning, flowering cycles, shape maintenance and blooming.

i believe i can split myself open, over and over, in papery spots of pink.

but i am speaking about prickly stems.

& a person could get used to salt.

About This Place

how the stocky man who showed up at 9:45 p.m. hoisted up my old mattress on his shoulders.

"i am mexican, i am strong," he said. "where are you from?" "turkey." "you are strong too."

how my mother's father lay on his deathbed, all sweetness.

how i listen to *disintegration* from start to end over and over again, forgetting about algorithms and context-less songs.

about my grandfather: i held his hands with latex gloves and pulled my mask down to smile at him. when i hugged him goodbye, he said "i will remember this embrace for the rest of my life."

the rest of his life, or the end of the month.

97 years on this earth is a nice long time.

in somatic experiencing, we discovered i have a lily pad on my stomach, roots shooting down to my pelvis. it used to be a swamp. i listened to the swamp and it moved out of me, took some space, became space.

the lily pad protects a dark mass.

how i need to learn to dance all over again.

how i smell of warm musk, carnation, red sandalwood and cassia.

how i say to myself, "this is the part of the dream that's going to be scary," but instead of turning around, i choose magical thinking. "if i break this raw spaghetti and throw it down the balcony, these red-eyed shadow cats won't appear in the wall across the alley."

i ride my bike to the turkish consulate. i take out my turkish id card, show it to a man who could play the piano but uses a keyboard instead. "i'm sorry, my turkish isn't so great," i say in turkish. "you cannot vote here, you are registered in turkey," he says.

i'm still there, though i haven't been in years.

my grandfather asked me where my heart was and i whispered the truth, for once. can't leave this plane without knowing there is love, even in absence.

the thought of my fallopian tubes gone was heartwarming this morning.

Hunger for the Divine

memory is a spirit caught in the low tide
and my mother's voice quick to warn,
"you can only adore god."
but what if the moon's pale white belly
were as deserving of my one beating heart?
as a woman grown it is easy to forget
how in the small of my lungs
i treasured a lone cooing dove,
sometimes
even adored it.
when someone i love enters the room,
let it be a long silk robe that i wear
as i wade through their waters.
what i mean to say is that we all need
another sun, clover honey, a breath of holy.

Inner Child Work

no one has ever told me, don’t go. or fixed
my tilted lampshade, changed the broken bulb.
you’re good, i want to hear. stay. you’ve made
it this far to stare at a heavy gold necklace
hanging from a fine needle. there’s the thread.
i’m glad you’re here. how about you lie on
this pile of woven blankets from denizli.
wrap yourself up. stare at this oil painting
of your mother. she was always so weary of it.
said her eyes were drawn sad. don’t go. stay.
you are a bloom. you draw your own eyes.
while you were resting, i changed the bulb.
i made it right. turn on the light. you’ll see.

NOTES

"Woman at a Window" is an ekphrastic poem inspired by Caspar David Friedrich's painting of the same name (1822).

"Exit Strategy" was inspired by elements from Ada Limón's poems "The Tree of Fire," "The Good Fight," and "Oh Please, Let It Be Lightning" from *Bright Dead Things* (Milkweed Editions, 2015).

The title "The World Begins Here" was inspired by Joy Harjo's poem "Perhaps the World Ends Here" from *The Woman Who Fell From the Sky* (W. W. Norton and Company Inc., 1994).

"The Marshmallow Experiment" refers to the seminal study on delayed gratification led by psychologist Walter Mischel at Stanford University in 1972.

"A Crack in Everything" borrows its title from Leonard Cohen's song "Anthem."

"After Breakfast" is an ekphrastic poem inspired by Elin Danielson-Gambogi's painting of the same name (1890).

The duplex poem "To Rewrite Memory" borrows three phrases from Bessel van der Kolk's *The Body Keeps the Score* (Penguin Books, 2015), namely "the extraordinary capacity of the human mind," "whether we remember a particular event at all" and "most day-to-day experience[s] pass[es] into oblivion."

"The Wounded Deer" is an ekphrastic poem inspired by Frida Kahlo's painting of the same name (1946).

"A Blue So Deep" is a response to Sarah Burgoyne's poem "Moon's Tresses," both published in *Frog Pond Review* (Issue 4, Fall 2023).

"Index" draws upon subcategories found under the "trauma survivors" index entry from Bessel van der Kolk's *The Body Keeps the Score* (Penguin Books, 2015), namely "flashbacks," "freeze response," "handwriting," "helplessness," "hypersensitivity to threat," "immune system," and "intimacy as [in] difficult."

"Foreshadowing" is an ekphrastic poem inspired by a self-portrait by Francesca Woodman from her *Space²* series (1976).

"Tell Me What You Know About Dismemberment" is a response to Bhanu Kapil's poem "Twelve Questions" from *The Vertical Interrogation of Strangers* (Kelsey Street Press, 2001). More specifically, the poem responds to the ninth verse, "Tell me what you know about dismemberment."

"Multiple Mirrors" was inspired by Patricia Renée Ewing's poem of the same name from *The Other Land* (Éditions Bonsecours, 1974).

In "Tongue Stories," the phrase "here we are tongue-tied before we collide" is taken from the song "Tongue Tied" by The Antlers.

The title "Île-Aux-Tourtes Bridge Partially Reopened Friday Morning, Additional Lane Opens Monday" was taken from a CBC headline published on May 30, 2021.

In “Tango Injuries,” the phrase “my one wild and precious life” is borrowed from Mary Oliver’s poem “The Summer Day” from *House of Light* (Beacon Press, 1992).

“Love’s Secret Domain” was inspired by and borrows its title from the Coil song of the same name.

In “Metamour,” the line “what’s so wrong with the light?” is taken from Angel Olsen’s song “Windows.”

“The Inn of the Dawn Horse” is an ekphrastic poem inspired by Leonora Carrington’s painting of the same name (1937-38).

In “Where Now?” the phrase “first, an idea of thorns, even in the absence of colour” was inspired by Nicole Brossard’s poems “The Inside of Someone: version2” and “The Inside: version3” from *White Piano*, translated by Robert Majzels and Erín Moure (Coach House Books, 2013).

Also in “Where Now?”: the line “the subtext: does this closure make me look open enough?” borrows its structure from a phrase in T. Liem’s poem “We Were Captioned Not Captured” from *Slows: Twice* (Coach House Books, 2023).

ACKNOWLEDGEMENTS

Some of these poems first found their form in writing workshops, where the facilitators generously offered their guidance, prompts, and insights. Heartfelt thanks to: the Quebec Writers' Federation, Carolyn Marie Souaid, Kasia Van Schaik, T. Liem, Fariha Róisín, Larissa Andrusyshyn, Sarah Wolfson, Poonam Dhir, Isabella Wang and Cassidy McFadzean.

Thank you to the editors of the following journals, where some of these poems, sometimes in earlier versions, first appeared: *Acta Victoriana, carte blanche, Eavesdrop Magazine, FreeFall Magazine, Frog Pond Review, Funicular Magazine, Headlight Anthology, LBRNTH, The Malahat Review,* and *yolk.*

Thank you to the team at Guernica Editions for your dedication and for helping make this collection a reality.

I am profoundly grateful to the wonderful souls whose belief, support, friendship and love breathed life into every word of this book. Thank you to Blue, so true. To Eric, Rex, C&C and the Schneewittchen. To Mustafa. To Oktay and Osman. To Safia and Malik. To my first readers, especially to Gage, Bibi, Denise, and Anne. To Xris, for helping me undo the score. And to my mother Micheline, whose bright spirit and Melek-eyes simply have no equal.

ABOUT THE AUTHOR

MERYEM YILDIZ is a poet born and based in Tiohtià:ke (Montreal) whose work has appeared in publications across Canada. In 2022, she won *The Malahat Review*'s Far Horizons Award for Poetry as well as the Quebec Writers' Federation's *carte blanche* Prize. With a background in psychology and translation, she draws deeply from the human experience and the complex interplay between language, culture and the psyche. *Backbone* is her first book.

Printed by Imprimerie Gauvin
Gatineau, Québec